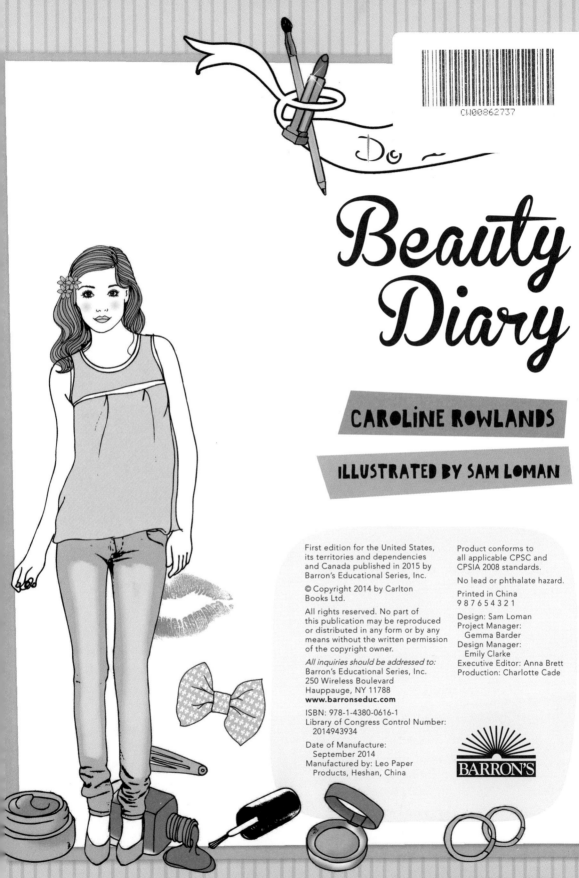

Beauty Diary

CAROLINE ROWLANDS

ILLUSTRATED BY SAM LOMAN

First edition for the United States, its territories and dependencies and Canada published in 2015 by Barron's Educational Series, Inc.

© Copyright 2014 by Carlton Books Ltd.

All inquiries should be addressed to:
Barron's Educational Series, Inc.
250 Wireless Boulevard
Hauppauge, NY 11788
www.barronseduc.com

ISBN: 978-1-4380-0616-1
Library of Congress Control Number:
  2014943934

Date of Manufacture:
  September 2014
Manufactured by: Leo Paper
  Products, Heshan, China

Product conforms to all applicable CPSC and CPSIA 2008 standards.

No lead or phthalate hazard.

Printed in China
9 8 7 6 5 4 3 2 1

Design: Sam Loman
Project Manager:
  Gemma Barder
Design Manager:
  Emily Clarke
Executive Editor: Anna Brett
Production: Charlotte Cade

BARRON'S

HOW TO USE THIS BOOK

This **DO IT YOURSELF BEAUTY DIARY** is the perfect accessory for beauty and style queens everywhere.

WHAT'S INSIDE?

- Jam-packed with makeup tips and beauty secrets, this book has everything you need to become a beauty expert.

- Make your own stylish jewelry and hair accessories, improve your posture with easy exercises, and try some beauty-boosting recipes.

- There's also space for you to write about what beauty products you've tried and tested, and stylish looks you love on the "Your Beauty Routine" pages.

In addition to the book, you'll find a set of stencils between pages 78 and 79 to help you create stylish makeup and body art designs.

You can also customize your makeup and beauty accessories with cool fabric stickers found at the front of the book.

PLUS, discover your true skin tone and what makeup will suit your skin best with the handy press-out skin-tone swatch cards at the back of the book.

STICKERS

Customize a makeup bag, perfume bottle, and hairbrush with these fun stickers. Or use them to decorate the hair accessory and jewelry you designed on pages 20 and 56.

PRESS-OUT SKIN-TONE SWATCH CARDS

Ever get confused about which makeup colors suit you best? Press-out the skin-tone swatch cards to find the perfect makeup for your skin tone, then check out pages 24, 26, and 30 for tips on how to apply it flawlessly.

STENCILS

Complete your look with these stylish stencils. Turn to page 78 for some pretty makeup ideas and body art designs.

READ ON TO DISCOVER BEAUTY TIPS AND STYLE SECRETS TO CREATE A LOOK YOU'LL LOVE.

MY BEAUTY ROUTINE

"My Beauty Routine" pages are a chance for you to write about your beauty routine; what you like to wear, what you eat, how you look after yourself, and all the makeup and style tips you've tried or would like to try.

WRITE about your month ahead here, what events you have coming up, and what beauty tips and tricks you are going to try out.

DRAW or stick pictures of your favorite celebrity's and friends' looks.

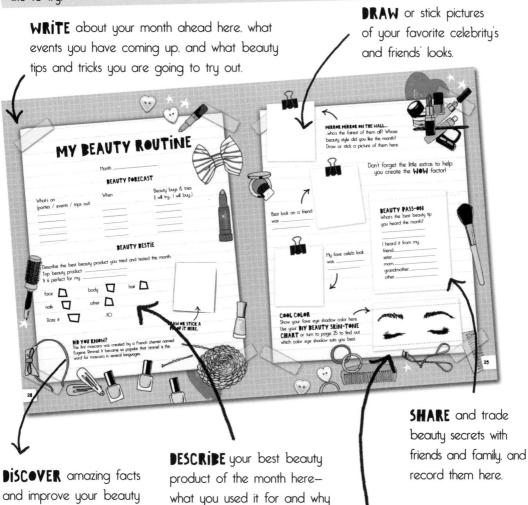

DISCOVER amazing facts and improve your beauty know-how.

DESCRIBE your best beauty product of the month here—what you used it for and why you like it.

DOODLE and color in the pictures to show what makeup shades and accessories suit you best.

SHARE and trade beauty secrets with friends and family, and record them here.

BEAUTY SECRETS

These pages offer all kinds of beauty advice, from what to eat to how to look after your skin, your hair, your nails, and your body. Packed with helpful hints and fun facts, you'll discover everything you need to know about feeling and looking great from head to toe, inside and out.

DISCOVER ways to help you look your best. All aspects of beauty are covered, including hair, skin, nails, and body.

BEAUTY KNOW-HOW, facts and advice will transform you into a beauty expert.

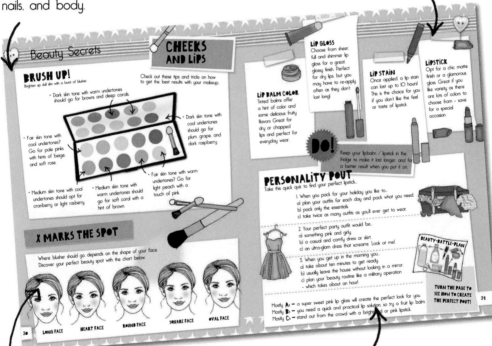

FUN QUIZZES will help you find the perfect look for you.

TRICKS AND TIPS will give you the confidence to try out new looks and products.

DO iT!

Practical and fun, these pages are bursting with ideas to make you look and feel beautiful, from healthy exercises and recipes, to easy craft makes. PLUS, there's lots of useful beauty techniques, from facials and manicures to applying makeup and shaping eyebrows.

GET HEALTHY with fun exercises and tasty recipes to try.

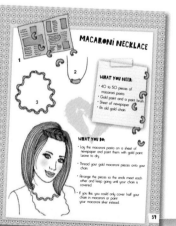

FOLLOW SIMPLE STEP-BY-STEP INSTRUCTIONS to make the most of your nails, skin, hair, and makeup.

COMPLETE YOUR LOOK with simple but stylish crafts.

Beauty Secrets

A pore is a tiny hole in your skin that allows your skin to breathe.

LOVE THE SKIN YOU'RE IN

5 SIMPLE RULES OF SKIN CARE

The secret to good skin care is to keep it simple...

1. **WASH** your face before you go to bed as dirt and makeup can clog your pores and irritate your skin.

2. **EXFOLIATE** your skin to remove dead skin cells and make your skin soft and smooth. To exfoliate your skin, you can use a hot washcloth or a facial scrub!

3. **MOISTURIZE** your skin to stop it from drying out— don't forget to wear a sunscreen on sunny days, too.

4. **EAT WELL**—take note of how your skin reacts to different foods and avoid the ones that make you blotchy!

5. Drink lots of **WATER**—dull-looking skin is often caused by dehydration. Water helps it stay soft and fresh.

BEST FOODS FOR YOUR FACE

Check out the notes below to find out what to eat and what to avoid for healthy skin.

Good...

FRUIT high in vitamin C will help your skin glow.

TOMATOES are packed with selenium which will protect your skin from the sun.

The vitamin E found in **HAZELNUTS** will help support healthy skin growth.

Eating oily **FISH** will help keep your skin supple and stop it from looking dry.

The zinc found in **CHICKEN** will help repair damage to your skin and keep it soft.

Not so good...

Too much **BREAD** and **PASTA** can clog your pores.

Having too much **SALT** on your food can cause your skin to puff up.

Too much **SUGAR** in your diet will age your skin.

Some say **CHOCOLATE** can irritate the skin, but if you can't resist it, opt for dark chocolate.

FRENCH FRIES and other foods cooked at high temperatures in hot oil can make your skin look dull.

6

SKIN TONE

Impress your friends
with some
skin-tone know-how...

- Skin comes in lots of different colors. These colors, also known as skin tones, are caused by your body's supply of a pigment called melanin. People with darker skin have more melanin than people with pale skin.

- Melanin kicks in to protect your body against the sun's UV rays, and is what causes your skin to tan. People with fairer skin produce less melanin than people with darker skin, so they tend to burn more easily.

- Understanding your skin tone will help you protect yourself from the sun's harmful rays and also find the right shades of makeup and clothing. Use your skin-tone swatches at the back of the book to find the best matches for you.

SKIN TONE CHART

Ivory   Apricot   Olive

Caramel   Deep Brown   Cocoa

SEE PAGE 56 TO FIND OUT WHAT COLOR JEWELRY SUITS YOUR SKIN TONE BEST.

SKIN DEEP

Your skin undertone is the color just beneath your skin. Take this quick quiz to find out what yours is, and what looks good with it...

1. In the sun you tend to...
a) burn easily
b) tan nicely

2. What color are your eyes?
a) blue, green, or gray
b) hazel, light brown, or dark brown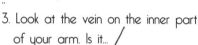

3. Look at the vein on the inner part of your arm. Is it...
a) more blue
b) more green

Mostly **As**—you're cool—you have red and pink undertones in your skin, so stick to silver, gray, green, and blue-red colors when choosing clothes and makeup.

Mostly **Bs**—you're warm—you have yellow, golden, and peach undertones in your skin, so look great in earth tones, such as gold, olive green, and orange-red based clothing and makeup.

DO!

If you want to color your hair, make sure you pick a color that matches your skin tone and undertone too!

DO IT! DIY FACIAL

MAKE YOUR FACE GLOW WITH A DIY FACIAL!

WHAT YOU'LL NEED:
- facial cleanser
- exfoliating scrub
- washcloth
- face mask
- moisturizer

2. Use your fingers to gently rub your exfoliating scrub all over your face. Use a circular motion and pay most attention to oily areas like your forehead, nose, and chin.

1. Clean all the dirt and makeup off your face, neck, and behind your ears using a facial cleanser.

3. Fill your bowl with warm water and soak your washcloth in it. Rinse it out and press it on your face for a minute or so. Repeat two or three times.

4. Apply your face mask (see opposite page for some great recipe ideas) and wash off after five to ten minutes.

5. Smooth a moisturizer over your face to finish.

WHY HAVE A FACIAL?

1. Cleansing the skin prevents skin irritation.
2. Exfoliating and removing dead skin cells from your skin will make it smoother and softer.
3. You'll feel relaxed and pampered!

Natural Beauty

MAKE YOUR OWN FACE MASKS AND CLEANSERS WITH THESE SIMPLE RECIPES...

Before applying anything to your face, always test a small amount on the back of your hand, to check that it doesn't irritate your skin.

• Mash up a **BANANA** and pat it onto your face to get a great treatment for dull and flaky skin.

• Combine 1/2 cup of hot water with 1/3 cup of **OATMEAL** or porridge and leave for two minutes. Mix in two table-spoons of plain yogurt, two tablespoons of honey, and one egg white. Apply a thin layer of the mask to your face and leave for 15 minutes before rinsing off with warm water.

• Mix 1 tablespoon of **NATURAL YOGURT** with the juice from a quarter of an **ORANGE** for a quick and easy face mask.

• Mash up an **AVOCADO** and mix with three tablespoons of cream and one tablespoon of honey. This will create a luxurious moisturizer that will leave your skin feeling great.

• For a quick cleanser, mix one table-spoon of **LEMON JUICE** and two cups of water as a finishing rinse to cleanse and tighten your skin.

Make sure you don't use any ingredients you are allergic to.

MY BEAUTY ROUTINE

Month ....

BEAUTY FORECAST

What's on (parties / events / trips out)	When	Beauty buys & tries (I will try... I will buy...)
....	....	....
....	....	....
....	....	....
....	....	....
....	....	....

BEAUTY BESTIE

Describe the best beauty product you tried and tested this month.

Top beauty product: ....

It is perfect for my: ....

face ☐   body ☐   hair ☐

nails ☐   other ☐

Rate it: ☐ /10

DRAW OR STICK A PICTURE OF IT HERE.

DID YOU KNOW?

Skin is the body's largest organ and makes up about 15% of your body weight.

Don't forget the little extras to help you create the **WOW** factor!

Get ultra stylish nails with a cool design—doodle one on the nails below.

BEAUTY PASS-ON

What's the best beauty tip you heard this month?

....
....

I heard it from my...
friend...
sister...
mom...
grandmother...
other...

THIS MONTH MY SKIN WAS...

normal ☑   blotchy ☐

greasy ☐   dry ☐

I ATE A LOT OF...

fruit ☐   chocolate ☐

potato chips ☐   vegetables ☐

SKIN DIARY

I DID THE FOLLOWING TO MY SKIN...

facial ☐   exfoliated ☐

moisturized ☑   cleansed ☑

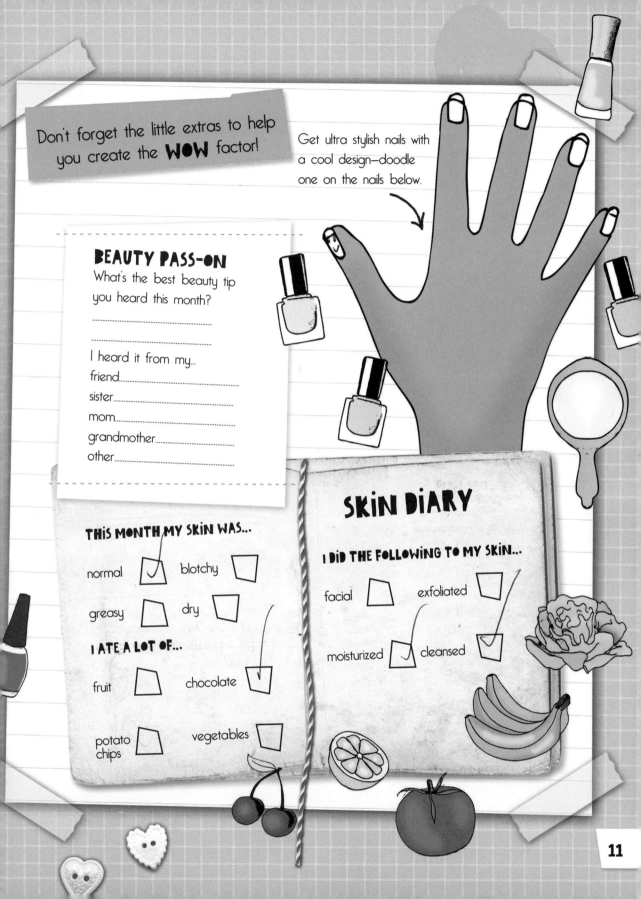

Beauty Secrets

HEALTHY HAIR

Find out how to keep your hair in tip-top condition and banish bad hair days forever!

HAIR CARE
When it comes to having luscious locks—it's not just about what you put on your hair but what you eat too!

DO!

Apply your hair products at least five minutes before you style, as this gives your hair a chance to absorb them, making them more effective.

1. Biotin, an ingredient used in shampoos and conditioner to make hair shine, can also be found in **EGGS**. Time to get cracking!

2. CHICKEN and other proteins will strengthen your hair and keep your scalp healthy.

3. CHOCOHOLICS take note—the vitamin B12 found in dark chocolate will help your hair grow.

4. A **FISHY DISH** is doubly good for you as it's packed with vitamin B12 and iron, which will stop your hair from falling out.

5. Super food **SPINACH**, has a healthy dose of zinc, which will make your hair stronger and even helps prevent dandruff.

CHOP CHOP!
Cutting your hair will not make it grow any faster, but cutting it every 8 to 12 weeks will make it look longer. A good cut will get rid of split ends, making your hair look thinner and shorter at the ends.

DON'T! Rub wet hair with a towel after you wash it—as it will make your hair frizzy. Instead, squeeze it and leave to air dry for a bit before you style.

WASH AND GLOW

Sometimes it's the simple things that matter in hair care... like washing it! So make sure you do it right.

1. When you cover your wet hair with shampoo, focus on the roots as this is where most dirt is.
2. Smooth the shampoo in, rather than rub or scrunch, as this will smooth the hair cuticles down.
3. After rinsing the shampoo off, apply conditioner, but this time focus on the mid lengths and ends of the hair, as these will be the most damaged.
4. Rinse your hair with cold water before you turn off the shower. This helps seal hair cuticles and prevent frizz.

WIDE-TOOTHED COMB

ROUND BARREL BRUSH

PADDLE BRUSH

VENT BRUSH

Turn the page to try out some fun and stylish hairstyles.

BRUSH STROKES!

Are you using the right hairbrush? Read on to find out...

A **PADDLE BRUSH** makes hair cuticles lie flat so is great for smoothing and detangling.

Use a **WIDE-TOOTHED COMB** to detangle knots in wet hair, as a bristly brush can damage it.

A **ROUND BARREL BRUSH** is the tool of choice for blow drying and creating bouncy curls.

The holes in a **VENT BRUSH** enable your hairdryer's heat to circulate at the roots to create more volume.

Hairstyles

Banish bad hair days forever with these quick and nifty hairstyles.

CREATE THE PERFECT BUN

1

- Select an old sock close to your hair color and cut off the toe end to create a tube.

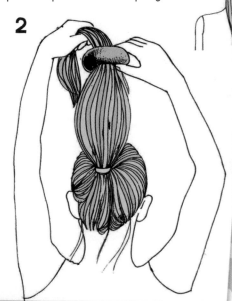

2

- Put your hair in a ponytail, then roll up the sock so it's a donut or ring shape and pull it over the ponytail.

BEST FOR LONG HAIR!

3

- Pull the sock donut to the end of your ponytail and start to roll up your hair over it, tucking it in while you roll.

4

- Slowly roll and tuck until you reach the base of your pony tail. Tidy up loose ends by using bobby pins around the base.

A FISHTAIL BRAID

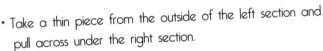

- Pull your hair into a ponytail and split into two equal sections.

- Take a thin piece from the outside of the left section and pull across under the right section.

- Take a thin piece from the outside of the right section and pull across under the left section.

- Keep going till you reach the end of your hair and secure with a hairband.

3

4

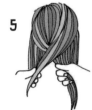

5

OVERNIGHT WAVES

1

- After washing your hair, blow-dry it so it's 80% dry.

- Divide into two sections and twist each section tightly, away from your face.

2

3

- Wrap each section around itself and secure with a hair band.

4

- Go to sleep and when you wake up in the morning, unravel each section, run your fingers through the waves and add some hairspray for extra hold.

MY BEAUTY ROUTINE

Month ....

BEAUTY FORECAST

What's on (parties / events / trips out)	When	Beauty buys & tries (I will try... I will buy...)
....	....	....
....	....	....
....	....	....
....	....	....
....	....	....

BEAUTY BESTIE

Describe the best beauty product you tried and tested this month.
Top beauty product: ....
It is perfect for my: ....

face ☐   body ☐   hair ☐

nails ☐   other ☐

Rate it: ☐ /10

DRAW OR STICK A PICTURE OF IT HERE.

DID YOU KNOW?

You get goosebumps when it's cold because your hair follicles get smaller, causing your skin to bunch up and hairs to stand on end.

Don't forget the little extras to help you create the **WOW** factor!

Color in these clothes to show what colors you've worn most this month.

MIRROR MIRROR ON THE WALL...
...who's the fairest of them all? Whose beauty style did you like this month? Draw or stick a picture of them here.

My fave celeb look was ....

Best look on a friend was ....

USE THE SPACE BELOW TO DRAW OR STICK SOME PICTURES OF HAIRSTYLES YOU'VE TRIED THIS MONTH AND RATE THEM.

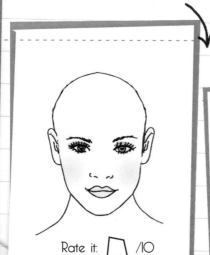

Rate it: ☐ /10

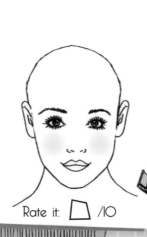

Rate it: ☐ /10

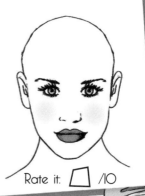

Rate it: ☐ /10

Beauty Secrets

YOUR HAIR

A CUT ABOVE

A good haircut can totally transform your look. Check out the face shapes below, find your match to discover which cut will suit you best.

OVAL

Any haircut will suit your face —from bobs, to pixie crops, to long layered locks. Lucky you!

LONG

Widen your face with a chin-length bob or cute bangs. Long hair will drag your face down, but if you do want it long, add some soft waves or curls.

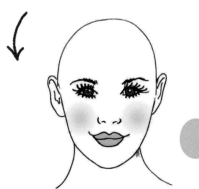
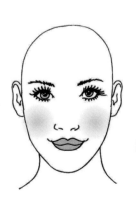
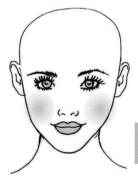
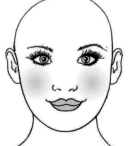

ROUND

Choose styles that will lengthen and frame your face. Long layers are good, but avoid a straight fringe or a short bob.

SQUARE

Try to soften your face with long layers that start just below your jawline. A side part will help too.

DO!

Choose a hairstyle that suits your personality and lifestyle. If you struggle to get out of bed in the morning, don't go for a haircut that needs lots of styling and might make you late for school!

18

HAIR FLAIR

When it comes to creating a specific look, up the style stakes with a carefully chosen hair accessory.

- Glam it up with some sparkly hair accessories.

- Nothing beats pretty flowers in the hair for Boho chic.

- For a fun and sporty style, pull your hair off your face with a ponytail holder and pop on a visor.

- Add a cute headband for a sweet and delicate look.

BUYING GUIDE

Follow these hair accessory dos and don'ts to make sure you shop smart.

DO!

- Match the accessory to the occasion. Sparkles and flowers are best for parties—while headbands help keep it casual.
- Contrast your hair accessory with your hair color to ensure it stands out.
- Do try on your new hair accessory before your planned event—some can be tricky to get right!

TURN TO PAGE 20 TO MAKE YOUR OWN UNIQUE HAIR ACCESSORIES!

DON'T

- Wear too many accessories at once.
- Buy loads of trendy hair accessories. It's fun to have a few, but make sure you also buy timeless accessories, like a black headband or a diamante barrette, that will last.
- Be afraid to try something new. Have fun experimenting with accessories you've never worn before—ask to borrow your friends' accessories so you can try before you buy.

DIY HAIR ACCESSORIES

1

2

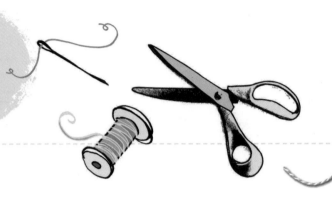

I. Take the two pieces of ric rac and glue or sew together at one end.

2. Lock in each curve of the first piece with the second, then wrap them over and under each other, like a braid, until the two lengths are locked together. Glue or stitch at the end to hold in place.

3. Take an end and start coiling it around itself. Put a little dot of glue every couple of centimeters.

4. When you have coiled it all, tuck the tail end behind and glue to secure in place.

5. Use your fingers to flip some of the petals outward.

6. Make as many as you like, then glue or stitch them to your headbands or barrettes.

6

3

4

5

RiBBON BOWS

MAKE THE PERFECT BOW ACCESSORY FOR YOUR HAIR.

WHAT YOU NEED:
Glue
Needle and thread
20 in. (50cm) of ribbon
Scissors
Buttons to decorate

1

1. Fold your ribbon in half and crease with your thumb, then lay flat. Bring one end of the ribbon to the center and lay on top of the crease, to form a loop.

2

2. Repeat the other end so your ribbon forms a figure eight, with two loops. Make sure your ribbon ends overlap.

3

3. Bring the outside edges of each loop into the center of the figure eight and pinch the center of the ribbon loops together.

4

4. Wrap a piece of thread around the middle and tie in a knot to secure. Sew or stick on a button for a great finishing touch.

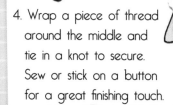

3 WAYS TO TRANSFORM A HEADBAND

1. Wrap colored threads around your band for an instant update.

2. Stick on some cute buttons for a quirky style!

3. Fresh or silk flowers give you a cute, hippy look. Use florist wire to attach them to your headband.

MY BEAUTY ROUTINE

Month ....

BEAUTY FORECAST

What's on (parties / events / trips out)	When	Beauty buys & tries (I will try... I will buy...)
....	....	....
....	....	....
....	....	....
....	....	....
....	....	....

BEAUTY BESTIE

Describe the best beauty product you tried and tested this month.
Top beauty product: ....
It is perfect for my: ....

face ☐   body ☐   hair ☐

nails ☐   other ☐

Rate it: ☐ /10

DRAW OR STICK A PICTURE OF IT HERE.

DID YOU KNOW?
On average, you lose 50 to 100 strands of hair a day.

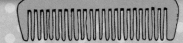

STYLE STATEMENT

Design some cute and cool hair accessories for the hairstyles below.

Color in the lips to show which color lip gloss or balm you've tried this month.

BEAUTY PASS-ON

What's the best beauty tip you heard this month?

....

....

I heard it from my...

friend..

sister..

mom..

grandmother................................

other..

ESSENTIAL KIT

A BEGINNER'S GUIDE TO MAKEUP

When it comes to makeup, working out what to wear and how to wear it can be a bit daunting, so check out these tips and tricks to get you started.

If you are new to makeup, you only need the basics in your makeup bag

- Eyes = mascara + eyeliner + eye shadow
- Face = tinted moisturizer + blush + concealer
- Lips = lip balm + lipstick + lip gloss

CREATE YOUR MASTERPIECE
You've got the kit... now you need to apply it!

1. Prep your skin by making sure it's clean and apply a good moisturizer.

2. Rub in your tinted moisturizer. If you have dark circles under the eyes, add a few dots of concealer to lighten.

3. Next come the eyes. Apply eye shadow, eyeliner, and then mascara—in that order.

4. Apply some colour to your lips with a lipstick, lip balm, or lip gloss.

5. Finish off with a light sweep of blush. Apply it to the apples of your cheeks, which are the round bits that pop out when you smile.

24

Finding the perfect eye shadow can be tricky, but the chart below will help you get it right.

BLUE

GREEN

BROWN

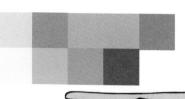

CLEAN UP!
Keeping your brushes clean is easy.

1. Run your brushes under lukewarm water, washing away all the makeup.
2. Fill a bowl with water and add a squirt of shampoo. Gently swirl your brushes in the water.
3. Rinse your brushes under running water again, until the water runs clear.
4. Use a cloth to pat your brushes dry and leave to dry completely overnight before using again.

TURN TO PAGE 30 FOR MORE MAKEUP TIPS AND TRICKS.

DON'T!

Use dirty brushes to apply your makeup. Clean and replace them regularly for the best results and to stop any skin irritations or infections.

BIGGER AND BETTER

Create the look of bigger. brighter eyes in **FiVE** easy steps.

1. Wearing two shades of eye shadow will really make your eyes pop. Use the darker color on the outer corner and the lighter shade on the inner one—then gently blend together.

2. Use white eye shadow near your tear ducts (inner corners of your eye) to brighten your eyes.

3. Dark eyeliner will make the whites of your eyes seem brighter and make your eyes look bigger.

4. Curl your eyelashes to open your eyes wider. Begin at the root of the lashes and hold the curler together for about 10 seconds. Then move the curler out to the end of your eyelashes and repeat.

5. Apply mascara by placing the wand at the base of your lashes. Sweep the wand up and repeat two or three times to get the thickness you require.

GRAB YOUR EYE MAKEUP STENCILS TO CREATE THESE COOL DESIGNS. USE EYELINERS, LiP LINERS, AND GLiTTER GEL FOR THE BEST RESULTS.

Turn to page 79 for tips and tricks on how to use them.

EYE TREATMENTS

WHAT TO DO

Place two cold cucumber slices over your eyes for five to ten minutes.

Soak two cotton balls in milk and place them over your eyes for five to ten minutes.

Place two teaspoons in the fridge overnight, then place them on your eyes for five minutes in the morning.

WHY DO IT

Cold cucumber slices contain antioxidants, that stop damage to skin cells and soothe irritated eyes.

Cold milk has a cool, calming effect on puffy eyes and its fat helps moisturize dry skin.

The cold metal will firm up your skin before you apply makeup.

SHAPE UP

All good makeup artists know that the eyebrows are an important feature on the face. They can lift the eyes and widen or narrow your face, so read on to get the best brows ever.

A—The inner edge of the eyebrow should line up with the outside of your nostril.

B—The highest point of your arch should be in line with the outer edge of your eyeball.

C—The outer edge of your eyebrow should finish here.

D—Get rid of any stray hairs, to create an arch above your eyelid.

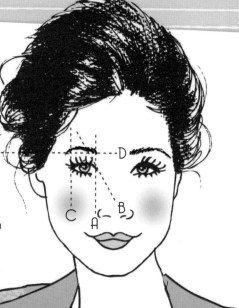

27

MY BEAUTY ROUTINE

Month ....

BEAUTY FORECAST

What's on (parties / events / trips out)	When	Beauty buys & tries (I will try... I will buy...)
....	....	....
....	....	....
....	....	....
....	....	....
....	....	....

BEAUTY BESTIE

Describe the best beauty product you tried and tested this month.
Top beauty product: ....
It is perfect for my: ....

face ▢   body ▢   hair ▢

nails ▢   other ▢

Rate it: ▢ /10

DRAW OR STICK A PICTURE OF IT HERE.

DID YOU KNOW?
The first mascara was created by a French chemist named Eugène Rimmel. It became so popular that "rimmel" is the word for mascara in several languages.

MiRROR MiRROR ON THE WALL...

...who's the fairest of them all? Whose beauty style did you like this month? Draw or stick a picture of them here.

Don't forget the little extras to help you create the **WOW** factor!

Best look on a friend was ....

BEAUTY PASS-ON

What's the best beauty tip you heard this month?

....
....

I heard it from my...
friend..
sister...
mom..
grandmother...............................
other...

My fave celeb look was ....
....

COOL COLOR

Show your fave eye shadow color here. Use your **SKIN-TONE CHART** or turn to page 25 to find out which color eye shadow suits you best.

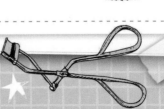

BRUSH UP!

Brighten up dull skin with a burst of blusher.

CHEEKS AND LIPS

Check out these tips and tricks on how to get the best results with your makeup.

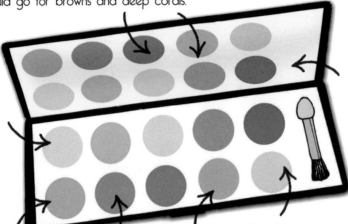

• Dark skin tone with warm undertones should go for browns and deep corals.

• Fair skin tone with cool undertones? Go for pale pinks with hints of beige, and soft rose.

• Dark skin tone with cool undertones should go for plum, grape, and dark raspberry.

• Medium skin tone with cool undertones should opt for cranberry or light raspberry.

• Medium skin tone with warm undertones should go for soft coral with a hint of brown.

• Fair skin tone with warm undertones? Go for light peach with a touch of pink.

X MARKS THE SPOT

Where blush should go depends on the shape of your face. Discover your perfect beauty spot with the chart below.

LONG FACE   **HEART FACE**   **ROUND FACE**   **SQUARE FACE**   **OVAL FACE**

LiP GLOSS

Choose from sheer, full and shimmer lip gloss for a great, glossy finish. Perfect for dry lips, but you may have to re-apply often as they don't last long!

LiP STAiN

Once applied, a lip stain can last up to 10 hours! This is the choice for you if you don't like the feel or taste of lipstick.

LiPSTiCK

Opt for a chic matte finish or a glamorous gloss. Great if you like variety as there are lots of colors to choose from—save for a special occasion.

LiP BALM

Tinted balms offer a hint of color and some delicious fruity flavors. Great for dry or chapped lips and perfect for everyday wear.

DO!

Keep your lip balm / lipstick in the fridge to make it last longer, and for a better result when you put it on.

PERSONALiTY POUT

Take this quick quiz to find your perfect lipstick…

1. When you pack for your vacation you like to…
   a) plan your outfits for each day and pack what you need.
   b) pack only the essentials.
   c) take twice as many outfits as you'll ever get to wear.

2. Your perfect party outfit would be…
   a) something pink and girly.
   b) a casual and comfy dress or skirt.
   c) an ultra-glam dress that screams: "Look at me!"

3. When you get up in the morning you…
   a) take about ten minutes to get ready.
   b) usually leave the house without looking in a mirror.
   c) plan your beauty routine like a military operation —which takes about an hour!

BEAUTY-BATTLE-PLAN

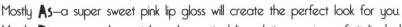

Mostly **A**s—a super sweet pink lip gloss will create the perfect look for you.
Mostly **B**s—you need a quick and practical lip solution, so try a fruit lip balm.
Mostly **C**s—stand out from the crowd with a bright red or pink lipstick.

TURN THE PAGE TO SEE HOW TO CREATE THE PERFECT POUT!

PERFECT POUT!

Make the most of your lips with these simple tips and tricks.

HOW TO APPLY LiPSTiCK

1. Apply a dab of lip balm to your lips, as dry and cracked lips won't hold color for long.

2. Outline your lips with a lip liner to stop your lipstick color from running. Pick one that is either the same shade or lighter than your lipstick color.

3. Apply a coat of your lipstick.

4. Finish with a shiny lip gloss or pat dry with a tissue for a chic, matte look.

THREE TiPS FOR HEALTHY LiPS

1. Exfoliate your lips by gently rubbing them with a dry toothbrush.

2. Polish your lips with some petroleum jelly or lip balm. For best results, wear overnight.

3. Drink plenty of water to prevent cracked and dry dehydrated lips.

1

2

3

LIPSTICK RULES!

DO

- Let your lips do the talking...opt for a bold and bright lip color and wear minimal makeup on your eyes and cheeks.

- Opt for a lip color darker than your skin, to avoid looking washed out.

- Match your makeup. If you are going for a neutral shade, keep the rest of your face natural, too.

DON'T

- Forget to brush your teeth before applying lipstick. Yellow teeth and bright lips are not a good look!

- Color your lips outside their natural shape, unless, of course, you're thinking of becoming a clown!

- Pick a shade just because it's fashionable. Find one that suits you, and you feel comfortable in.

THE CURSE OF THE COLD SORE

Cold sores can be painful and embarrassing, and they always show up at the worst times! Put a stop to painful cold sores with these simple tips.

- Keep healthy—cold sores strike when you are tired and your immune system is low. Eating well, exercising, sleeping, and drinking plenty of water will help fight off an attack.

- Protect your face and lips from the sun with lip balm and sun lotion.

- The amino acid arginine helps promote cold sore outbreaks —so avoid foods that are rich in this when you're feeling run down, like nuts, spinach, and (sadly) chocolate!

33

MY BEAUTY ROUTINE

Month ....

BEAUTY FORECAST

What's on (parties / events / trips out)	When	Beauty buys & tries (I will try... I will buy...)
....	....	....
....	....	....
....	....	....
....	....	....
....	....	....

BEAUTY BESTIE

Describe the best beauty product you tried and tested this month.
Top beauty product: ....
It is perfect for my: ....

face ☐   body ☐   hair ☐

nails ☐   other ☐

Rate it: ☐ /10

DRAW OR STICK A PICTURE OF IT HERE.

DID YOU KNOW?
The first lipsticks were made thousands of years ago, when women used to grind precious gems and decorate their lips with their dust!

Don't forget the little extras to help you create the **WOW** factor!

Best look on a friend was ....
....

MIRROR MIRROR ON THE WALL...

...who's the fairest of them all? Whose beauty style did you like this month? Draw or stick a picture of them here.

My fave celeb look was ....
....

You've nailed your hair and makeup... now design the perfect outfit.

LIP-TASTIC

Rate these lipstick colors with 1 for the best and 10 for the worst, to show your preference. ➔

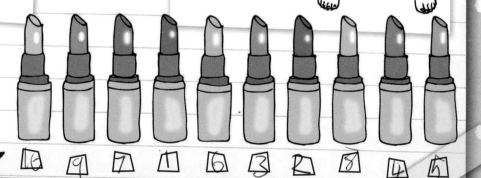

10 9 7 1 6 3 2 8 4 5

BODY BEAUTIFUL

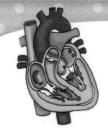 +  =

WORK IT OUT!

READ ON TO LOOK GREAT ON THE OUTSIDE AND FEEL GOOD ON THE INSIDE TOO!

Exercise is a great way to keep healthy and strong. Aerobic exercise like running, swimming, or dancing will get your heart pumping, which helps it get better at its main job—delivering oxygen around your body. Exercise is also scientifically proven to put you in a good mood. When you exercise, your brain releases chemicals called endorphins that make you feel happy. So what are you waiting for? On your marks, get set, go!

HOW TO GET PERFECT POSTURE...

Good posture can make you look and feel more confident (and prevent knee, back, and hip pain when you are older). Get it right in **THREE** easy steps.

1. Sit up straight by uncrossing your legs and planting your feet on the floor. Your neck and head should be in line with your spine.

2. When you stand, make sure you balance your weight between each foot, relax your shoulders, and pull your belly button toward your spine.

3. Don't text while you walk—it can affect your movement and stability. It also forces you to hunch over which is bad for your spine (plus you might bump into a lamppost!).

DO!

Make sure you drink plenty of water after exercise to help you rehydrate.

SKIN SECRETS

Keeping your skin soft and supple is easy when you know how...

1. Warm water is best for cleaning your skin. Just make sure it's not too hot as this can irritate your skin.

2. Gently pat, rather than rub, your face dry with a clean towel so you don't pull on your skin.

3. Exfoliate before you moisturize, as this will remove dead skin cells, clearing the way for your moisturizer to do its job.

4. Always moisturize your skin after a bath or shower—this helps lock in the moisture and stops your skin from drying out.

5. Your elbows and knees may need an extra rub with moisturizing cream, as they can dry out easily.

6. Always protect your skin in the sun. Slip on a hat, slop on a T-shirt and slap on some sun lotion to keep it healthy. Use sunscreen on cloudy days, too!

BODY ART

Turn your body into a work of art with your tattoo stencil sheet. Impress your friends with these cool designs.

TURN THE PAGE FOR SOME FANTASTIC YOGA POSITIONS TO KEEP YOUR BODY TONED AND CHILL YOUR MIND.

DO iT! BODY BALANCE

Take time out each day to relax your mind and strengthen your body with these easy yoga moves.

1. MOUNTAIN POSE

How to do it:

Stand with your feet hip-width apart and your arms by your side. Breathe deeply and evenly as you raise your arms up and stretch them toward the sky.

WHAT DOES iT DO? Improves your posture.

HOW HARD iS iT? Easy peasy.

2. DOWNWARD FACING DOG

How to do it:

Get on your hands and knees and walk your hands forward. Straighten your legs. so your body makes an upside-down V shape.

WHAT DOES iT DO? Great for stretching your calves.

HOW HARD iS iT? Quite easy.

3. WARRIOR POSE

How to do it:

Stand with your legs apart. Turn out your right foot 90° and your left foot in slightly. Stretch your arms out with your palms down. Lunge into your right knee.

WHAT DOES iT DO? Strengthens and stretches your legs and ankles.

HOW HARD iS iT? Takes a bit of practice.

4. TREE POSE

How to do it:

Start in the mountain pose. then shift your weight onto your left leg. Place the sole of your right foot inside your left thigh and find your balance. Bring your hands into a prayer position. Repeat on the other leg.

WHAT DOES iT DO? Improves your balance.

HOW HARD iS iT? Practice makes perfect.

5. COBRA POSE

How to do it:

Lie on the floor with your hands underneath your shoulders, legs extended and the tops of your feet on the floor. Push up and lift your chest off the ground.

WHAT DOES IT DO? Strengthens spine, arms, and wrists.

HOW HARD IS IT? Takes a bit of practice.

6. BOAT POSE

How to do it:

Sit on the floor with your legs straight in front of you. Lean back, lifting your legs. Stretch your arms to the front, with your palms facing your body.

WHAT DOES IT DO? Strengthens spine and tummy.

HOW HARD IS IT? Practice makes perfect.

7. SEATED FORWARD BEND

How to do it:

Sit on the floor and slowly bend your body toward your knees, with your head down and arms outstretched. Only go as far as feels comfortable.

WHAT DOES IT DO? Helps relieve stress.

HOW HARD IS IT? Takes a bit of practice.

8. EASY POSE

How to do it:

Sit up straight, on the floor, with your legs crossed in front of you. Rest your hands on your knees.

WHAT DOES IT DO? Aligns and strengthens your spine.

HOW HARD IS IT? Easy peasy!

MY BEAUTY ROUTINE

Month ....

BEAUTY FORECAST

What's on (parties / events / trips out)	When	Beauty buys & tries (I will try... I will buy...)
....	....	....
....	....	....
....	....	....
....	....	....
....	....	....

BEAUTY BESTIE

Describe the best beauty product you tried and tested this month.
Top beauty product: ....
It is perfect for my: ....

face ☐   body ☐   hair ☐

nails ☐   other ☐

Rate it: ☐ /10

DRAW OR STICK A PICTURE OF IT HERE.

DID YOU KNOW?
Wearing the wrong shoes can damage your spine.
Pick comfy shoes that will support your spine and body.
Save heels for special occasions!

Don't forget the little extras to help you create the **WOW** factor!

My fave celeb look was ....
....
....

Best look on a friend was ....
....

BEAUTY PASS-ON
What's the best beauty tip you heard this month?
....
....

I heard it from my...
friend...
sister...
mom...
grandmother...
other...

MIRROR MIRROR ON THE WALL...
...who's the fairest of them all? Whose beauty style did you like this month? Draw or stick a picture of them here.

DESIGNER DOODLES
Draw some body art designs below (find your stencils between pages 78 and 79).

HOW TO KEEP YOUR NAILS STRONG

Check out these top tips on how to grow strong, healthy nails.

DO

- Eat a well-balanced diet. Nails are made of protein, so add to their strength by eating lots of chicken, fish, and spinach.

- Do get regular manicures (turn to page 44 to find out how!).

- Moisturize your hands every time you wash them.

- Wear gloves when it's cold to stop your nails and hands from becoming dry and damaged.

NAIL IT!

If you're guilty of a bit of nail-nibbling, read on for tips and tricks on how to get perfect nails.

DON'T

- Don't cut your cuticles as they protect your nails from infection—push them back instead.

- Don't use nails as tools to open letters... use a pair of scissors, or a letter opener.

- Don't peel off old polish. It will damage your nails. Always use a nail polish remover.

- Never file back and forth. File your nails from the outside edge to the center so you don't weaken them.

ALMOND   **STILLETO**   **SQUARE**

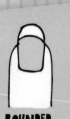  

ROUNDED   **SQUOVAL**   **OVAL**

HOW TO SHAPE YOUR NAILS

- Pick a shape you like.
- Take a nail file and file your nails from the outside edge to the center.
- Only file in one direction, and only file when your nails are dry.

PERFECT POLISH

Polishing your nails has never been so much fun—experiment with polish, glitter, and nail stickers to create the coolest designs. Try these clever tips and tricks on your nails!

1. Use a bit of netting to create this nifty effect on your nails.
- Paint your nails with a base coat and let it half dry.
- Place a small piece of netting (or you can use a piece of fishnet tights) over the nail and sponge on a second color or glitter. Leave to dry, then peel off netting.

Do!

Layer up nail polish colors to make your nails look longer.

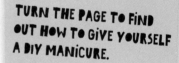

TURN THE PAGE TO FIND OUT HOW TO GIVE YOURSELF A DIY MANICURE.

2. Glam up your nail design by dipping half-dry nails in a pot of glitter.

3. Use a toothpick to create a pretty heart-shape on your nails.
- Dip your toothpick into your pot of nail polish and create a dot.
- Place a second dot next to it.
- Add a third dot underneath it.
- Use your toothpick to blend the dots together to form your heart.

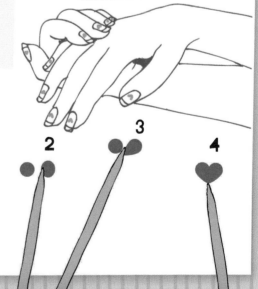

1   2   3   4

DO iT!

DIY MANICURE

Keep your nails in tip-top condition by doing this simple manicure once a week!

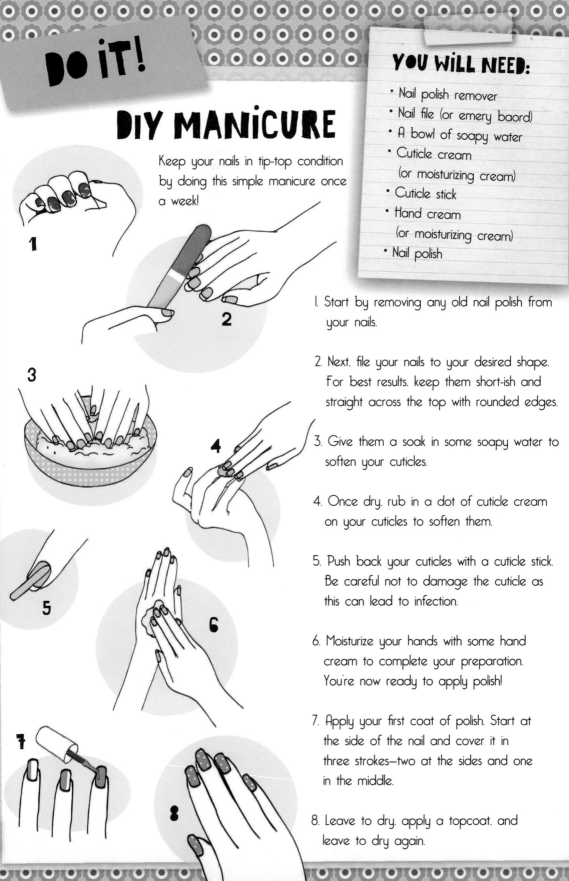

YOU WiLL NEED:

- Nail polish remover
- Nail file (or emery baord)
- A bowl of soapy water
- Cuticle cream
  (or moisturizing cream)
- Cuticle stick
- Hand cream
  (or moisturizing cream)
- Nail polish

1. Start by removing any old nail polish from your nails.

2. Next, file your nails to your desired shape. For best results, keep them short-ish and straight across the top with rounded edges.

3. Give them a soak in some soapy water to soften your cuticles.

4. Once dry, rub in a dot of cuticle cream on your cuticles to soften them.

5. Push back your cuticles with a cuticle stick. Be careful not to damage the cuticle as this can lead to infection.

6. Moisturize your hands with some hand cream to complete your preparation. You're now ready to apply polish!

7. Apply your first coat of polish. Start at the side of the nail and cover it in three strokes—two at the sides and one in the middle.

8. Leave to dry, apply a topcoat, and leave to dry again.

PRACTICE MAKES PERFECT!

Once you've nailed a simple manicure, why not try out these cool nail designs? Don't forget to have your nail polish remover handy, as some are a bit tricky and will take a couple of tries to get right.

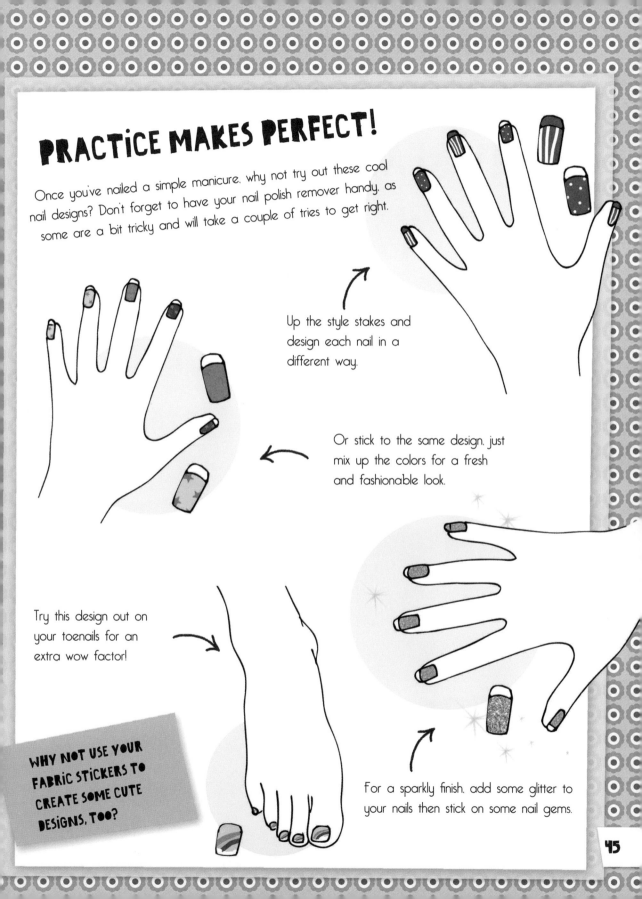

Up the style stakes and design each nail in a different way.

Or stick to the same design, just mix up the colors for a fresh and fashionable look.

Try this design out on your toenails for an extra wow factor!

WHY NOT USE YOUR FABRIC STICKERS TO CREATE SOME CUTE DESIGNS, TOO?

For a sparkly finish, add some glitter to your nails then stick on some nail gems.

MY BEAUTY ROUTINE

Month ....

BEAUTY FORECAST

What's on (parties / events / trips out)	When	Beauty buys & tries (I will try... I will buy...)
....	....	....
....	....	....
....	....	....
....	....	....
....	....	....

BEAUTY BESTIE

Describe the best beauty product you tried and tested this month.
Top beauty product: ....
It is perfect for my: ....

face ☐   body ☐   hair ☐

nails ☐   other ☐

Rate it: ☐ /10

DRAW OR STICK A PICTURE OF IT HERE.

DID YOU KNOW?

Your nails are made of the same stuff as your hair—keratin—
which means the foods that are good for your hair, will give you
strong and healthy nails, too.

Don't forget the little extras to help you create the **WOW** factor!

BEAUTY PASS-ON
What's the best beauty tip you heard this month?
....
....

I heard it from my...
friend...
sister...
mom...
grandmother................................
other...

Doodle some pretty earrings to make the most of an up-do!

PERFECT POLISH
Rate these nail colors with 1 for the best and 10 for the worst. to show your preference.

YOU ARE WHAT YOU EAT

No matter how hard you try, if you don't feel good on the inside you won't look good on the outside. Read on to discover healthy-eating secrets that will help you look (and feel) great.

EAT YOURSELF BEAUTIFUL

The key to being healthy and looking good is to eat a balanced diet. Use the chart below to make sure you're eating the right amount of each food group.

REVIVE WITH FIVE!

Eating at least five portions of fruit and vegetables a day is a great way to keep healthy and stay beautiful. Try these nifty ways to get your five a day!

1. Add some chopped bananas or berries to your morning cereal.
2. Make your own smoothies, packed with yummy fruit and calcium.
3. You don't have to eat just fresh vegetables. A portion of canned baked beans will do the job, too.
4. Use fruit or veggies when you bake —add zucchini or carrots to your cakes, or berries and raisins to your cookies. Yum!
5. Swap a sandwich for a delicious veggie soup.

BEAUTY BOOSTERS

Some foods are better for you than others. Read on for what to munch on to help you look your best.

1. Inside just one almond nut you'll find skin-boosting zinc and hair- and bone-strengthening calcium.
2. Spinach will boost the collagen in your skin, making it look and feel better.
3. Tuck into pumpkin to strengthen your nails.
4. Bananas are high in potassium, which will help get rid of tired eyes.
5. The antioxidants in green tea will help give you a great complexion.

SAY CHEESE!

Lipstick may help create the perfect pout, but for a truly great grin, you need to take care of your teeth and gums too.

- Brush and floss twice a day. Using a fluoride toothpaste will also help harden your teeth and prevent decay.
- Milk, greens, and almonds are packed with calcium, which will keep your teeth and gums healthy.
- Opt for water over sugary and acidic drinks, like carbonated drinks and fruit juices.
- Casein protein, found in cheese, will strengthen your teeth.
- Chew on raw veggies, as this helps produce lots of saliva to fight germs in your mouth and prevent bad breath.

DO!

Try a tasty coconut. Its high levels of Omega 3 and essential fatty acids will help your hair grow and keep your skin soft and supple.

WATER WORKS

Water makes up around half of your body weight and helps you fight off illness and carry blood around your body. Staying hydrated keeps your brain alert and active and your skin looking great. So make sure you drink a glass or two of water with every meal and snack, plus extra when it's hot outside.

TURN THE PAGE FOR SOME SCRUMPTIOUS RECIPES.

EAT WELL

SALMON PASTA

(serves 4)

WHAT YOU NEED:

- 7 oz. (200g) pasta
- 7 oz. (200g) salmon
- 6 tablespoons of crème fraîche
- 1 can of chopped tomatoes
- A handful of grated cheese (Parmesan is best)
- A pat of butter

Grab your apron and chopping board for quick and easy recipes that taste great and are good for you too!

WHAT TO DO:

- Cook the pasta in a large pan of water, according to the instructions on the package (ask an adult to help).
- Wrap the salmon in some foil with a pat of butter and cook in the oven at 350°F (180°C) / Gas Mark 5 for 15 to 20 minutes.
- Heat the crème fraîche and the chopped tomatoes in a pan, stirring until blended. Add the cheese, stir until melted then remove from heat.
- Remove the salmon from the oven, break it up into small, bite-size pieces and add it to your sauce. Be careful when you do this, as the salmon will be hot!
- Drain the pasta and toss together with your sauce. Delicious!

WHY IT'S GOOD FOR YOU:

Salmon is an excellent source of protein, vitamins, and minerals. However, its main benefit is that it's good for your heart as oily fish helps blood flow freely around your body. Crème fraîche is a healthy alternative to full-fat cream and tastes just as good.

LITTLE EXTRAS!

Add some chopped spinach to your sauce for an extra boost of iron. It will help keep your hair healthy and strong.

DON'T FORGET TO ASK AN ADULT TO HELP YOU COOK THE PASTA AND USE THE OVEN.

WHAT TO DO:

- Mash the avocado and mix in the grated cucumber.
- Add the rest of the ingredients and mix well.
- Transfer to a bowl and serve with chopped peppers, carrots, celery, or steamed asparagus.

WHY IT'S GOOD FOR YOU:

Avocadoes are a great source of lutein, which works as an antioxidant and prevents eye disease. They also contain vitamins and folic acid that will help keep your heart healthy.

AVOCADO DIP

WHAT YOU NEED:

- 1 ripe avocado
- ⅓ of a cucumber, peeled and grated
- 2 tablespoons of low-fat yogurt
- Juice of ½ lemon
- Cayenne pepper

BLUEBERRY SMOOTHIE

WHAT YOU NEED:

- 2.5 oz. (75g) blueberries
- 1 banana
- 100ml of apple juice

WHAT YOU DO:

- Add the ingredients to a blender and mix together to make a delicious smoothie. If you don't have a blender, mash up the fruit with a fork, then add the apple juice.

WHY IT'S GOOD FOR YOU:

Blueberries are a superfood and are packed with antioxidants, which help stop damage to your body's cells. They're also said to improve your memory, so snack on them while you study for a test!

MY BEAUTY ROUTINE

Month ....

BEAUTY FORECAST

What's on (parties / events / trips out)	When	Beauty buys & tries (I will try... I will buy...)
....	....	....
....	....	....
....	....	....
....	....	....
....	....	....

BEAUTY BESTIE

Describe the best beauty product you tried and tested this month.

Top beauty product: ....

It is perfect for my: ....

face ☐   body ☐   hair ☐

nails ☐   other ☐

Rate it: ☐ /10

DRAW OR STICK A PICTURE OF IT HERE.

DID YOU KNOW?

If you're looking for a superfruit to munch on, go for a blackberry. It's the fruit with the highest levels of antioxidants and is bursting with vitamins and potassium.

MIRROR MIRROR ON THE WALL...

...who's the fairest of them all? Whose beauty style did you like this month? Draw or stick a picture of them here.

BEAUTY PASS-ON

What's the best beauty tip you heard this month?

....

....

I heard it from my...

friend...

sister...

mom..

grandmother...............................

other...

Best look on a friend
was ....

....

Don't forget the little extras to help you create the **WOW** *factor!*

My fave celeb look
was ....

....

Dish of the day

SUPERFOOD!

The healthiest dish I ate this month was:

....

Draw a picture of it here.

ESSENTIAL EXTRAS

1. Bright skinny belts look great over a cardigan.

2. Wrap a scarf around your waist to update an old dress.

3. Braid some string, ribbons, or rope together to create a cool nautical-style belt to wear with your jeans.

BELT UP!

A belt is a great way to update an old outfit or add a stylish finish to a new one.

HEADS UP!

Top off your look with a stylish hat—just make sure you pick the right one for your face shape!

SQUARE: Choose hats with a floppy or curved brim to help soften your face.

ROUND: Try a fedora! The height and brim are great for your face shape.

OVAL: You look great in all kinds of hats, but avoid tall and narrow ones.

BRiNG ON THE BLiNG!

Jewelry is a great way to give your look the wow factor. Try these easy tips and tricks for how to use your bling to draw attention to your hair, eyes, and clothes.

- If you want to appear taller, opt for a long necklace. Try a choker necklace to make you seem shorter.

- Long dangly earrings will lengthen a round face, while studs or smaller earrings are best for those with long or oval faces.

TURN TO PAGE 6 TO FiND OUT WHETHER YOUR SKiN TONE iS WARM OR COOL.

- Gold jewelry looks best on warm-toned skin, while silver will enhance cooler tones.

DON'T

Overload your look with too much clutter. Pick just one part of your face and one part of your body you want to highlight. Too many accessories could look messy.

PiERCED EARS

If you've just had your ears pierced (or are hoping to have them done!) read on for three top tips on how to look after them.

1. Make sure your first earrings have a gold post (the part that slips through your ear) as this will be less likely to cause infection.
2. You will need to leave your first earrings in for up to six weeks, until the holes have healed. That way they won't close up when you remove your earrings.
3. Keep your newly pierced ears clean by keeping them clean and rubbing antibiotic ointment on them.

DO iT!

MAKE YOUR OWN ACCESSORIES

Try these quick and easy makes to create some cool accessories to complete your look.

WHAT YOU NEED:

- Paper towel or toilet paper roll
- 1 yd. (1 m) of colored ribbon
- Duct tape (or other sticky tape)
- Scissors
- Glue
- Sparkly sequins and gems (optional)

COOL CUFF BRACELET

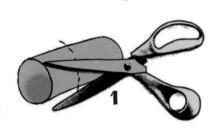
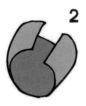

WHAT TO DO:

- Cut a section off your paper roll, as wide as you want your cuff bracelet to be.
- Cut down the middle of the cut-off piece.
- Wrap the cuff in duct tape for extra strength.
- Add a spot of glue and stick the end of your ribbon to the inside of the cuff.
- Tightly wrap the ribbon around the cuff until it is covered. Then cut off any extra ribbon and glue the end of the ribbon to the inside of the cuff.
- For extra sparkle stick on some gems or sequins.

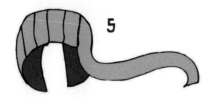

MACARONI NECKLACE

1

2

3

WHAT YOU NEED:

- 40 to 50 pieces of macaroni pasta
- Gold paint and a paint brush
- Sheet of newspaper
- An old gold chain

WHAT YOU DO:

- Lay the macaroni pasta shapes on a sheet of newspaper and paint them with gold paint. Leave to dry.

- Thread your gold macaroni pieces onto your chain.

- Arrange the pieces so the ends meet each other and keep going until your chain is covered.

- If you like, you could only cover half your chain in macaroni, or paint your macaroni silver instead.

MY BEAUTY ROUTINE

Month ....

BEAUTY FORECAST

What's on (parties / events / trips out)	When	Beauty buys & tries (I will try... I will buy...)
....	....	....
....	....	....
....	....	....
....	....	....
....	....	....

BEAUTY BESTIE

Describe the best beauty product you tried and tested this month.

Top beauty product: ....

It is perfect for my: ....

face ☐   body ☐   hair ☐

nails ☐   other ☐

Rate it: ☐ /10

DRAW OR STICK A PICTURE OF IT HERE.

DID YOU KNOW?

Diamonds are formed over billions of years under intense pressure and heat, deep underground. They are sometimes brought to the Earth's surface by volcanic eruptions!

Don't forget the little extras to help you create the **WOW** factor!

Doodle a cute pattern on the belt below.

MIRROR MIRROR ON THE WALL...
...who's the fairest of them all? Whose beauty style did you like this month? Draw or stick a picture of them here.

Doodle some sparkly gems or a pretty pendant to complete this necklace.

Best look on a friend was ....
....

My fave celeb look was ....
....

SPARKLY STYLE
Design a perfect piece of jewelry...
Will it be:
earrings ⬠ a ring ⬠ a necklace ⬠ a bracelet ⬠
gold ⬠ silver ⬠ rose gold ⬠ white gold ⬠

SCENTS-ATIONAL!

Picking the perfect scent can be tricky, but a little know-how goes a long way!

TYPES OF FRAGRANCE

EAU DE TOILETTE—this type of fragrance contains between 5–15% of essential oils or extracts, but it's quite weak and the scent won't last that long because it's diluted with water.

EAU DE PARFUM—is slightly stronger, using between 10–20% of aromatic oils. It's more potent and lasts longer than eau de toilette.

PARFUM—this is the longest-lasting fragrance, using more than 20% of aromatic essence. It packs a potent punch so should be dabbed, rather than sprayed on.

FRAGRANCE FAMILY

A fragrance family chart is used to describe different scents. There are four main categories—woody, fresh, floral, and oriental. A mixture of all four of these categories is called a Fougère.

STRAIGHT TO THE POINT
Follow these simple steps on how to apply your perfume.

1. Spray or dab your perfume onto your pulse points, which are the locations in your body where your blood vessels are closest to your skin. These spots radiate heat that will help the fragrance spread from your skin into the air. Your pulse points are on the inner wrists, at the base of your throat, inner elbows, and behind your knees and ears.
2. Do not rub your wrists together after applying, as this can crush the scent!
3. Apply your perfume before putting on your clothes as it can stain some fabrics.

Apply some petroleum jelly to your skin before applying your perfume, as it will make your perfume last longer!

WHAT'S YOUR FRAGRANCE PERSONALITY?

Take this quick quiz to find out...

1. After school you love to...
a) get stuck into your homework
b) relax in the garden and get some fresh air
c) eat a healthy snack of fruit and veggie
d) just chill out

2. Your friends describe you as...
a) reliable and realistic
b) a bit of a dreamer
c) outgoing and active
d) laid-back and easygoing

3. Which fashion style do you like best?
a) smart and clean
b) flirty and floaty
c) sporty and fresh
d) cool and casual

4. Which kind of smell do you love the most?
a) fresh air
b) flowers and fresh-cut grass
c) citrus fruits like lemon and orange
d) home-baked cookies

TURN THE PAGE TO MAKE YOUR OWN PERFUME TO MATCH YOUR SCENT STYLE.

Mostly **As**—an oriental perfume will add a bit of spice and keep you fresh.

Mosty **Bs**—a floral scent will reflect your emotional and dreamy personality best.

Mostly **Cs**—a fruity fragrance will complement your fun-loving and active lifestyle

Mostly **Ds**—a light, natural and woody scent matches your laid-back attitude.

DO IT!

MAKE YOUR OWN PERFUME

WHAT YOU NEED:

- 2 teaspoons of almond oil
- Essential oils of your choice —orange, lavender, and peppermint are good ones to start with
- A small lump of beeswax
- An old lip-balm pot

SOLID PERFUME

WHAT TO DO:

1

- Combine about 2 teaspoons of almond oil with your essential oils. Add a drop or two of your essential oils at a time, until you have the scent you like.

2

- Melt a small chunk of beeswax in a glass dish in the microwave.

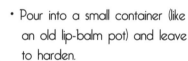

4

- Pour into a small container (like an old lip-balm pot) and leave to harden.

3

- Once melted, add the oil mixture and stir to combine.

DON'T FORGET TO ASK AN ADULT TO HELP YOU MELT THE BEESWAX.

LiQUiD PERFUME

WHAT YOU NEED:

- A handful of rose petals
- A handful of lavender leaves/flowers
- A saucepan
- 1 bottle
- 2 cups of water
- A sieve

WHAT TO DO:

- Gently wash your rose petals, lavender leaves, and flowers to remove any dirt.

- Add 2 cups of water to a saucepan and bring to a boil. Ask an adult to help you with this part.

- Turn off the heat, add your petals to the water, then leave to cool.

- Use a sieve to strain the contents away from the water and put the water in a pretty bottle.

- Think of a name for your perfume and decorate your bottle with a label and colorful ribbon.

1

2

3

4

5

Eau de Rose

MY BEAUTY ROUTINE

Month ....

BEAUTY FORECAST

What's on (parties / events / trips out)	When	Beauty buys & tries (I will try... I will buy...)
....	....	....
....	....	....
....	....	....
....	....	....
....	....	....

BEAUTY BESTIE

Describe the best beauty product you tried and tested this month.

Top beauty product: ....

It is perfect for my: ....

face ☐   body ☐   hair ☐

nails ☐   other ☐

Rate it: ☐ /10

DRAW OR STICK A PICTURE OF IT HERE.

DID YOU KNOW?

It's official—perfume can make you feel better! Experts have linked scent to emotion. so try a lavender scent to help you relax or a lively citrus one for an instant energy boost.

MIRROR MIRROR ON THE WALL...

...who's the fairest of them all? Whose beauty style did you like this month? Draw or stick a picture of them here.

BEAUTY PASS-ON

What's the best beauty tip you heard this month?

....
....

I heard it from my...

friend...
sister..
mom...
grandmother...................................
other..

Best look on a friend

was ....

....

My fave celeb look

was ....

....

Don't forget the little extras to help you create the **WOW** factor!

INVENT YOUR OWN PERFUME...

What would it smell of...

Give it a name ....

Design a bottle for it here:

BEAUTY SLEEP

Everyone knows you feel better after a good night's sleep, but getting the right amount of sleep will help you look better too.

DREAM HOURS

When you're a baby, you need up to 18 hours of sleep a day. By the time you're a teenager, this has dropped to about nine hours. Sleep needs can vary from person to person, so it's important to recognize how much sleep YOU need to feel (and look) your best.

SEVEN STEPS TO SLEEP

Follow these simple steps to getting a good night's sleep:

1. Eat and drink well during the day and get plenty of sunshine and fresh air.

2. Eat your final meal at least three hours before you go to bed, so you don't go to sleep feeling too full or needing the bathroom.

3. Create a bedtime ritual; this could be a warm shower or bath, reading a book, or listening to soothing music. These will then acts as triggers, telling your body that sleep is on its way.

4. Take a tech-break from your computer and phone screen before your head hits the pillow. Writing a to-do list will help you de-clutter your mind.

5. Spray soothing scents around your room—lavender and jasmine are very relaxing.

6. Make sure your mattress is comfy and your bedroom dark and cool.

7. Try going to bed and getting up at the same time every day— to regulate your body clock.

TURN TO PAGE 68 FOR MORE GREAT IDEAS TO HELP YOU SLEEP.

BEAUTY-BOOSTING BENEFITS

Sleep is nature's most powerful beauty treatment.

When you're tired, your blood doesn't flow as effectively, which can deprive your cells of oxygen, stop cell growth, and make your skin look dull. When you sleep, your skin renews itself and your facial muscles relax—so a good night's sleep helps your skin look softer and fresher.

DO!

Combine your beauty sleep routine with a sleepover and invite your friends over for an overnight pamper party! See page 72 for some great pamper party ideas.

SLEEPING BEAUTY

Nighttime is the perfect time to pamper yourself, so try these overnight beauty tips and tricks while you sleep.

• Sleep on a satin pillow to reduce hair breakages and frizz.
• Braid your hair before you go to sleep and unravel it in the morning for natural waves.
• If your hair suffers from a serious lack of bounce, wash and dry it before bedtime and go to sleep in soft rollers. Just remember to take them out before you leave for school!
• Get rid of dry skin on your feet and hands by smothering them in moisturizing cream and going to sleep with gloves and socks on.
• Reduce dark under-eye circles (caused by fluid build up under the eye), by raising your head up with a puffy pillow while you sleep.
• Apply any creams that have brightening ingredients in them like retinol or vitamin C at night as sunlight can stop them from working to their fullest potential.
• Sleeping on your back will enable your back and neck to rest in a natural position and improve your posture.

WHAT YOU NEED:

- Fabric 1—8 x 4.5 in. (20 x 12cm)
- Fabric 2—8 x 4.5 in. (20 x 12cm)
- Black felt—8 x 4.5 in. (20 x 12cm)
- Length of elastic
- Scissors
- Needle and thread
- Template—look!

SWEET DREAMS

Try these great makes to help you snooze in style.

1

SLEEP MASK

If counting sheep isn't working, slip on this blackout sleep mask for a perfect night's sleep.

2

3

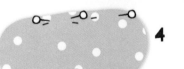

4

5

WHAT TO DO:

1 Copy the sleep mask pattern above and cut it out to create a template. You'll need to make it a bit larger to cover your eyes.

2 Use your template to cut out one piece of outer fabric and one piece of reverse fabric. Then cut out a slightly smaller piece of felt.

3 Pin your fabrics together, so the pretty side of fabrics 1 and 2 are facing each other and sew the edges together. Leave one of the shorter sides unsewn.

4 Turn the mask inside out and insert the black felt lining. Then pin the remaining edges together and neatly sew up.

5 To finish, remove the pins and sew a length of elastic to either side of the mask and you'll be ready to snuggle down and catch some zzzzzzs!

LAVENDER BAG

Sweet dreams are guaranteed when you pop this lavender bag inside your pillowcase.

WHAT YOU NEED:

- 2 fabric pieces 3.5 x 6 in. (10 x 15cm)
- 6 in. (15cm) ribbon
- 1 bunch of dried lavender
- Scissors
- Needle and thread

WHAT TO DO:

Remove the flowers from your dried lavender.

1

2

Pin your fabric pieces so the pretty sides are facing each other.

3

Sew the fabrics together along the two longer sides and shorter bottom side. to create a sachet bag. leaving the top open.

4

Turn the sachet bag right side out and carefully spoon your lavender into it.

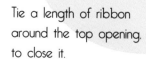

5

Tie a length of ribbon around the top opening. to close it.

MY BEAUTY ROUTINE

Month ....

BEAUTY FORECAST

What's on (parties / events / trips out)	When	Beauty buys & tries (I will try... I will buy...)
....	....	....
....	....	....
....	....	....
....	....	....
....	....	....

BEAUTY BESTIE

Describe the best beauty product you tried and tested this month.
Top beauty product: ....
It is perfect for my: ....

face ☐   body ☐   hair ☐

nails ☐   other ☐

Rate it: ☐ /10

DRAW OR STICK A PICTURE OF IT HERE.

DID YOU KNOW?

If it takes you less than five minutes to fall asleep at night you might be sleep deprived, as it should take ten minutes.

Design some cool sunglasses to finish off your look.

Doodle a bangle you'd like to buy in the box below.

DREAM DECODER

Figure out what your dreams mean with the explanations below.

FLYING DREAMS

Dreaming of flying means you are feeling confident and secure about your life and totally in control. If you worry that you are flying too high in your dream, it sometimes means you are worried about how your success will change you and your life.

FALLING DREAMS

If you dream you are falling, either from the sky or from a cliff or down a hole, this can mean you feel out of control. Try to work out what area of your life you need to take control of and what you can do and these dreams will stop.

DREAMING THAT YOU CAN'T TALK

Dreaming you can't speak can often mean you are afraid to tell people what you think and to voice your true opinions. A good way to solve this problem is by writing down your thoughts, then slowly, over time, you will build up the courage to say what you think.

PARTY TIME

Throw the perfect pamper party for you and your friends.

Create your guest list here. Try to stick to under eight people as you don't want your beauty room to be too crowded, and go for an even number of guests to make sure everyone has a pamper partner to try out treatments on.

MY PLAYLIST

GUEST LIST

TOP TUNES

Choose relaxing music to chill out to while you have your treatments. Make a playlist here of your fave songs.

SNACK ATTACK

Make sure you've got plenty of snacks to munch on. Check out the snack and smoothie recipes on page 51 for some tasty beauty-boosting ones!

PAMPERING SESSIONS

Divide your night into slots where you can try out different beauty treatments. You could try: face masks, manicures, pedicures, hair styling, and some relaxing yoga moves. Mix and match and double up on treatments, so one friend could be painting another friend's nails while her face mask is on. Then remove her mask while her nails dry.

FUN AND GAMES

Have a laugh with your friends while you beautify yourselves by playing some fun games:

GUESS THE SCENT: Fill five bottles with some essential oils and see which friend names them correctly.

CELEBRITY SKIN: Print off some pictures of your fave celebrities and see if you can figure out if they have warm or cool skin tones.

REAL OR FAKE TREATMENTS?: Have your guests guess which beauty treatments are real and which are fake. From fish nibbling your feet to exfoliate them, to mud and bird-poo face masks. You'll need to make up some fake ones too!

BEAUTY QUIZ: Put together some of the quizzes in this book (look at pages 31 and 61) to test your friends' beauty know-how.

GOODY BAGS

Don't forget to give your friends a goody bag to take home. You could fill them with the homemade perfume, face masks, and accessories you can make in this book.

Eau de Rose

PiCTURE PERFECT

Now that you've got your beauty look all sorted out—make sure you take some great pictures of yourself to share with your friends and family.

HOW TO TAKE A GREAT SELFiE:

Follow these simple rules to getting the best shot.

1. Download a photo app on your phone that will help you create your masterpiece.

2. Choose a favorite outfit that makes you feel comfortable. If you feel good, you'll look good!

3. Make sure you get the light right. Step outside and early morning or late afternoon is the best time to take your picture.

4. Pick your location and check out what's behind you—you don't want anyone or anything photo-bombing your picture!

5. Don't pout—just smile naturally, be brave, and show your teeth.

6. Either look directly at your phone/camera or look at another point and pretend you're having a conversation with someone, even if no one else is around.

THAT'S iT—YOU'RE DONE!

74

POSING TIPS AND TRICKS

Whether you're taking the shot or posing for a cameo—check out what to do and why. You'll then take great pictures of you and your friends.

DO! Practice your pose in front of a mirror.

DO! Roll your shoulders back as this will make your neck longer.

DO! Take your camera or phone everywhere. Practice makes perfect and the more photos you take, the better your pictures will be.

DO! Position your arms away from your body and rest your hands on your hips—this will make you look relaxed and natural.

DON'T! Forget the little things. A dirty mark or a tangled necklace can ruin a shot.

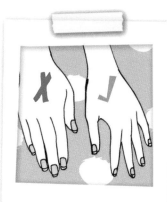

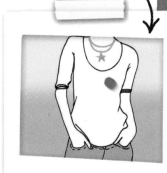

DON'T! Wear patterned clothes. Keep it plain and simple so your face stands out, not your clothes.

DON'T! Clump your fingers together as this will make your hands look big.

75

MY BEAUTY ROUTINE

Month ....

BEAUTY FORECAST

What's on (parties / events / trips out)	When	Beauty buys & tries (I will try... I will buy...)
....	....	....
....	....	....
....	....	....
....	....	....
....	....	....

BEAUTY BESTIE

Describe the best beauty product you tried and tested this month.
Top beauty product: ....
It is perfect for my: ....

face ☐   body ☐   hair ☐

nails ☐   other ☐

Rate it: ☐ /10

DRAW OR STICK A PICTURE OF IT HERE.

DID YOU KNOW?

One of the most expensive beauty treatments in the world is a gold leaf facial, where pieces of gold are rubbed into the skin to improve the complexion.

TIMELESS BEAUTY

Does your beauty routine run like clockwork. or is it a bit more random?
Fill in the chart below to get the lowdown on your beauty habits.

How often do you...	Twice a day	Every day	Once a week	Twice a week	Once a month	Never	Other
Wash your hair?							
Brush your teeth?							
Get a haircut?							
File your nails?							
Polish your nails?							
Exfoliate?							

PERFECT PICTURES
Stick your best selfies and pictures of friends here.

BEAUTY ESSENTIALS

Add the wow factor to your look with your stencils, stickers, and skin-tone swatch cards.

SKIN-TONE SWATCH CARDS

Become a beauty expert by using these cool press-out cards to find the perfect hair and make-up colors to suit your skin tone. Then invite your friends over to help them figure out theirs, too.

Turn to page 30 for clever blush tips.

Experiment with different colors to find the perfect combination for you.

BEST...

APRICOT

EYE SHADOW: light brown, blue, lilac, and green.
BLUSH: rose pink.
LIP COLOR: apricot shades, rose pink, and coral

Use two or more eye shadow colors to really make your eyes pop!

BEAUTY STICKERS

These cute stickers will look great stuck on your:

• make-up products
• jewelry box
• makeup bag
• beauty accessories

Or use them to decorate the pages of the book.

78

BODY ART STENCIL SHEET

Use your stencil designs to create these stylish make-up and body art designs.

STENCIL TIPS

1. Carefully cut around your stencil shapes to separate them from each other—this will make them easier to hold up to your face or body when stencilling.

2. Make sure that the decorative and makeup products you are going to use to create your designs won't harm your skin and are easy to remove. Eyeliner, blush, and lip gloss work really well.

3. Try out your stencil designs on a piece of paper first. Practice makes perfect!

4. Use a sponge rather than brush to apply color for larger stencil areas.

5. If you are using two colors, let the first one dry before applying the second, to avoid the colors merging.

Stencil some sweet hearts in a row around your ankle to create a cute anklet. Turn to page 56 to create some other cool accessories.

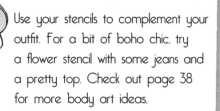

Add some sparkle to your eye makeup with some glittery stars. See page 28 for tips and tricks on how to make your eyes shine.

Use your stencils to complement your outfit. For a bit of boho chic, try a flower stencil with some jeans and a pretty top. Check out page 38 for more body art ideas.

BEAUTY ROUNDUP

It's official—you are now a beauty expert! Fill in the page with your best beauty tips, tricks, buys, and tries...

MY TOP THREE BEAUTY BESTIES

1. ....
....
2. ....
....
3. ....
....

My fave hairstyle looks like this...

MY TOP THREE ACCESSORIES

1. ....
....
2. ....
....
3. ....
....

Color in the face to show your fave eyeshadow, blush, and lipstick colors.

Number these scents from 1 to 3, in order of preference...

fruity

flowery

spicy